From the Desk of His Holy Eminence

Don't let them sell you any of that evolution bullshit.

Ireisum...

Darling,

You're an educated woman now which means your father **and you** can be privy to my mesmerizingly complex geopolitical views. We'll do lunch.

Babs

Babs

PRIME MINISTER
BENJAMIN NETANYAHU

Settle the West side of your room at all costs!
— *Netanyahu*

John Howard • Prime Minister

Don't let those college boy bastards get you down. Raise your head high and send it smashing into his nose, driving it into his brain, killing your man instantly.

Cheers, luv

John Howard

SYDNEY 2000

PRIME MINISTER HASHIMOTO

Dear Lazy,Walking-In-House-With-Shoes Chelsea-San,

Your inferior, stupid education system makes me want to sick. Still, have good time.

U.S.S.R.
~~UNION OF SOVIET SOCIALIST REPUBLICS~~
RUSSIA

Enclosed please find a gift certificate to Krazy Vaklav's World of Liquors Enjoy college!

Boris

Socks

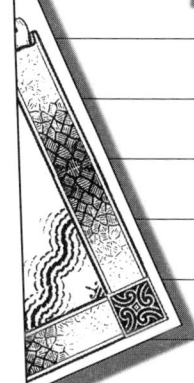

Office of Campus Life

STANFORD UNIVERSITY

Dear Student,

Welcome, Class of 2001! You have just taken your first step into a wonderful tapestry, comprised of many threads of colors and ideas. Stanford is much like a grand, oaken loom wherein the young minds within this bedazzlingly fibrous panorama may intertwine, enriching each other, all the while remaining distinct; capable of fashioning anything from a sombrero to a sweat-sock. Now you have an opportunity to sew your own little ideas into our ever-growing pattern. It is up to you to decide what to become: a jockstrap or a cummerbund.

Now, as we all know, the First Daughter, Chelsea Clinton, will be one of our merry, little threads. While we are all excited, we want to emphasize that there will be **NO** special treatment of <u>anyone</u> on this campus. Those of you who become Chelsea Clinton's "friends" will be treated NO better than those of you whom she finds unclean. In order to ensure conformity/equality, we have installed the following rules:

1. Avert your eyes when addressing Chelsea.
2. You may only speak to Chelsea if she addresses you. If Chelsea addresses you, you must abandon all conversations in which you are currently involved to properly deal with Chelsea's request, statement, or sigh.
3. If you address Chelsea, she does not have to pay you any attention, but the Secret Service may use the universal language of violence to answer your undesired verbosity.

Good luck and remember to have fun. I'll see you on Mandatory Friendship Day. Attendance <u>will</u> be taken.

Best Wishes,

Francis Gibson

Francis Gibson
Junior Dean of Campus Life

Not too late to <u>transfer</u>!

MANDATORY FRIENDSHIP DAY

"The Love You Take = The Love You Make"

10:00 Breakfast Bonfire for the Rain Forests
12:30 Lunch: slice of pizza and a soda on the Wilbur Hall Lawn
- choice of plain or pepperoni
- Find a Pizza-buddy!!!

2:30 Frosh will be stranded in the wild hills of Palo Alto with a match, a compass, and some felt. Make it back by sundown.
- Find a Survival-buddy!!!

7:30 Dr. Hypnowski: The Mad Polish Hypnotist
8:30 A Cappella Jamboree
9:30 "You + Sobriety= FUN" Dance
- Find a Dance-buddy!!!

11:00 Lockdown in Arriliga Gym. <u>SLUMBER PARTY</u>! Ghost stories, s'mores indoors and much, <u>much</u> more.

Get <u>transfer</u> application!

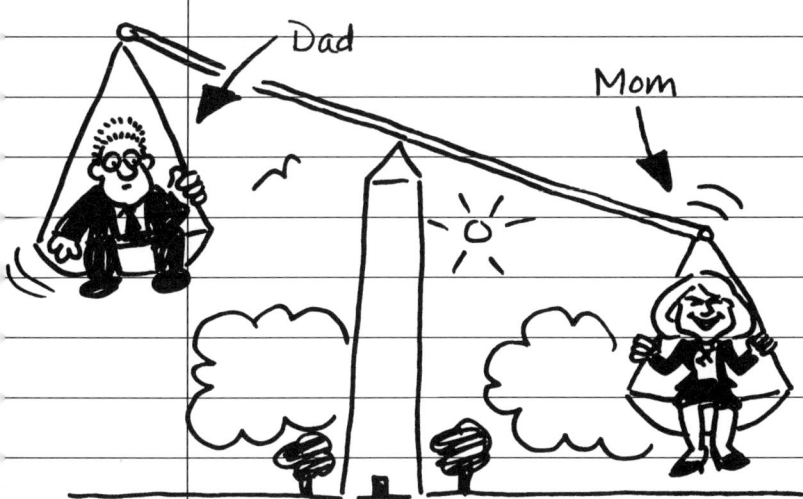

Dad

Mom

The Balance of Power

To Do List

1. Check e-mail
2. Laundry (don't forget fabric softener)
3. Change Chelsea robot's wig to match new haircut
4. Buy new extension cord
5. Set up secret meeting betw'n Arafat & Netanyahu; negotiate treaty
   * — let Dad know this time!
6. Get milk

Socks

English		Prof. Gobang	10:00 am	TR
American	History	Prof. Schmaltz	2:30 pm	MW
Anthropology		Prof. Pfaltzgraff	12:30 pm	TR
Dance Class		Eva Borgikov	5:30 pm	MW
Art History		Prof. Decré	10:00 am	MW

ANTHRO☺

Prof. Pfaltzgraff

ANTHROPOLOGY 143   (1st Class)

<u>Question:</u> What is anthropology?

<u>Answer:</u> studies the development of human culture.

Example: a lack of significant body hair drives man to craft tools to cope with the cold and environment.

● **PROGRESSION:**

Socks w/sax

A. 45,000 years ago, Neanderthal side scrapers used to fashion hides.

B. 11,000 years ago, Azilian needles provide for more sophisticated fur clothing.

C. 5 years ago, spray-on hair achieved.

Wait a minute! I'm gonna be in the encyclopedia! I didn't even have to do anything!

```
                                    C
                                  C H
                                C H E L
                              C H E L S
                            C H E L S E
                          C H E L S E A
                            H E L S E A
                            E L S E A
                            L S E A
                            S E A
                            E A
                            A
```

English	Prof. Gobang

Newt was here!

HIERARCHY OF LITERATURE

Banned books
Anything by Shakespeare
Epic poems involving Ancient Mariners
Epic poems involving Middle-Aged Mariners
Books
Manifestos
Dirty Limericks
Car rental agreements
Literary criticism
Limericks
Shampoo directions
Screenplays

So, Tony, if you have to take a bullet for Dad, do you have to take a bullet for me?

I'll have to check on that.

The lucky bastard who kidnaps me is gonna be RI-ICH!

DEATH TO ALL PAPARAZZI!!

Socks

CVCVCVC
VCVCVCV
CVCVCVC

Need Loft for Room—
Think International

EIFFEL TOWER

may be
too tall—
check ceiling
height

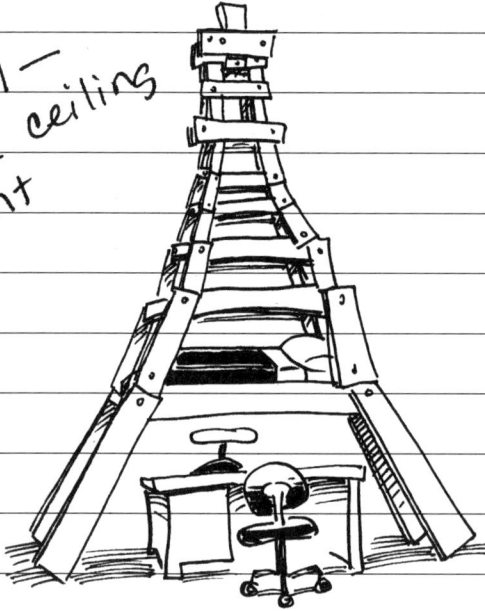

Battlement
are sex

MEDIEVAL CASTLE

could attract
bugs

LONDON BRIDGE
(might fall down?)

POLYNESIAN HUT

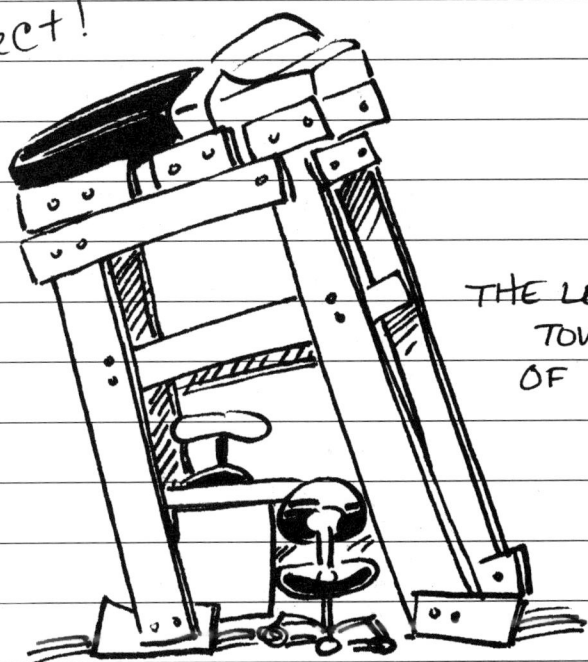

VICE PRESIDENT

HILLARY RODHAM CLINTON

EAST WING
WHITE HOUSE
1600 PENNSYLVANIA AVENUE
WASHINGTON D.C.

Hi Sweetie,

Just got off the phone with you and I forgot to mention that we decided to send you that shredder we talked about. Chelsea, it's never too early to start learning good habits.

Glad you and your roommate liked the package I sent with your Dad's "special" brownies. They're OK to eat, as long as you don't digest them. Ha, ha.

Speaking of your Dad, he wanted me to ask you what he should do about that darn Middle East problem. He liked how you wrapped up Bosnia, and would really like you to figure out this Israel thing as soon as possible. I know you said not to put the hit on Arafat, but he's really getting on Dad's nerves, and you know how hot-headed your father can be.

The White House feels empty and so, so lonely. Socks certainly misses you. All he does is pace around, pawing at the furniture, and licking his ass. As for your father and I, we're trying to cope with the loneliness by renting out your room. There's a nice little Chinese gentleman there right now. Don't worry though honey, he'll never be able to fill your shoes.

Oops, gotta go, your father's gotten into the baco-bits again. He's like a blood hound with those things, I swear.

Love,

Mom

P.S. Feel free to use this letter to test out your new shredder.

dictated but not read (HC/je)

Art History   Prof. Decré

may I call you Chel? ☺

No. ☹

Matisse (1869-1954) French

-Fauvism- decadently ~~jajeune~~ in its bacchanalian evocation of paint

- **very** gauche but wise in the rhythmic assemblage of shape, light, hues, motifs, color, nudists

- pithily witty in its savagely civil undulations

boring ☹

Are you going to pledge a sorority, Chel?

No.

Have you thought about ΔΔΔ?

No.

I think you'd be perfect for ΔΔΔ. How about coming by the ΔΔΔ house and meeting some of the ΔΔΔ girls?

NO!

How about the ΣΧ mixer?

Sit somewhere else.

Thursday   Slept through English class. Get notes.

I'm like a pair of magnets

Chelsea
Clinton

CVC
100
5 100
100

I'm so bored. Do you want to hear some National Secrets?

Sure

– Nixon not dead. Alive and well and living in San Fran w/ Ford.

– We **never** had nukes – BIG bluff.   KA-B

Loophole in Declaration of Independ– U.S. still legally part of England

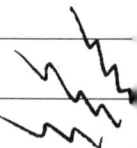

the MEN of Sigma Chi coridally invite you to attend...

ΣX

ENTER

ΣX's

11th Annual
"You Bring It—Our Pledges'll Eat it" Party

Bring who you want. Bring what you want.

But if you want to keep it,
keep it away from our
pledges' mouths!

Door prises awarded for the most disgusting item. Put on your thinking caps to beat last year's winner (the pus burger of death)!

Awards presented by reigning champ, Jake "E. coli" Weintraub & runner-up Vince "Medical Waste" Ignowski

TRI-DELT

Everything I needed to know for college I missed when I skipped the third grade:
• – Naptime
• – Maturity level of a nine-year old
• – 3rd Grade Annual Reefer Fest

AMERICAN HISTORY 101
Prof. Shmaltz

Washington's crossing of the Delaware, Xmas 1776, resulted in capture of 1,000 soldiers at Trenton, NJ
— Americans forced POWs to consume British foods and listen to whole pgs. of <u>Tess of the D'Urbervilles</u>

CVC **cvc**

<u>Camp Valley Forge</u> — cold, hungry, trapped by the winter of '77, a young George Washington quells mutiny by entertaining men with a <u>**fabulous**</u> coconut halves and grass skirt dance number

* Hail to the Beef!

Have you thought about becoming a ΔΣ sister??

No.

You should. You'd really fit in well.

No.

Y'know, Aretha Franklin was a ΔΣ. So was Lena Horne — and Carol Moseley-Braun

Aren't you a black sorority?

We can change.

NOTE: for Poli-sci— check if there is show & tell. If so, get Dad.

PROPOSED SECURITY ROOM: AREA 92

THE NEW CLOSE-QUARTERS SECURITY ROOM FOR THE 1998 SEASON PROVIDES, IN ADDITION TO ITS ARRAY OF STATE-OF-THE-ART DEFENSE MECHANISMS, A LAUNCHING SYSTEM ENABLING THE ENTIRE ROOM TO EJECT FROM THE BUILDING SHOULD ITS SAFETY BECOME COMPROMISED. THIS ROOM HAS BEEN CUSTOMIZED TO MEET THE SPECIFIC NEEDS OF TODAY'S ACTIVE COLLEGE STUDENT.

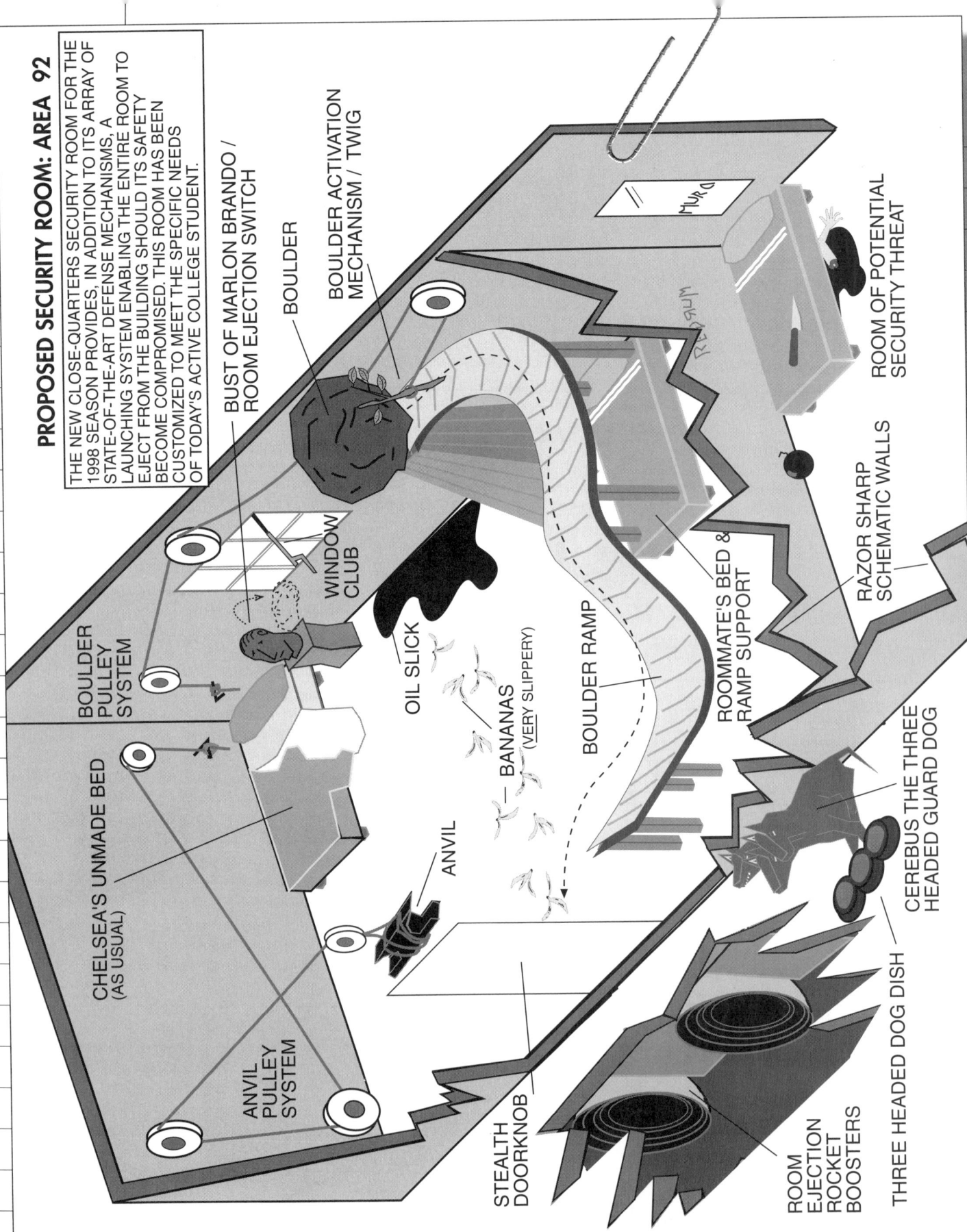

BUST OF MARLON BRANDO / ROOM EJECTION SWITCH

BOULDER

BOULDER ACTIVATION MECHANISM / TWIG

ROOM OF POTENTIAL SECURITY THREAT

BOULDER PULLEY SYSTEM

WINDOW CLUB

OIL SLICK

BANANAS (VERY SLIPPERY)

ROOMMATE'S BED & RAMP SUPPORT

RAZOR SHARP SCHEMATIC WALLS

CHELSEA'S UNMADE BED (AS USUAL)

ANVIL

BOULDER RAMP

CEREBUS THE THREE HEADED GUARD DOG

ANVIL PULLEY SYSTEM

STEALTH DOORKNOB

ROOM EJECTION ROCKET BOOSTERS

THREE HEADED DOG DISH

Tony, are you NUTS? My roommate's not sleeping under a boulder!

yadda, yadda, yadda, yadda

ANTHRO 143 Continued

Social-cultural anthro continued from last class:

- Humans use ~~tools~~ to improve the diet, aiding not only the acquisition of food, but preparation for consumption.

- **PROGRESSION:**

A. 350,000 years ago, simple choppers developed for hacking animal flesh

B. 13,000 years ago, specialized stone harpooons aid fishing

C. 40 years ago, spork technology perfected. Consumption simplified. People rejoice.

D. 10 years ago, container engineered to keep the hot side hot and the cold side cold.

HOT SIDE   COLD SIDE

Chelsea Clinton
Chelsea Clinton

Hey Tony, I was wondering if you could do me a favor?

Depends

Seeing as it's Friday and all I was wondering if you could buy me some beer?

What's this word?

Beer?

No way. I answer to the President.

I thought we had one of those priest/confession privacy things...

Nope

Washington Post headline:
First daughter Busted Buying First Beer, Prez Blames Tony.

Foreign or Domestic?

LUNCH TIME!
12

Bio 101

Off with their heads!

The Gore Girls
The Bore Girls
The Snore Girls
The Store (bought) Girls
The Open Sore Girls
~~The Dork~~

****

If I had a prehensile tail (the grippy kind)

I could:

* Pat head while rubbing tummy
(finally!!)

* Get it pierced to piss off
Mom and Dad

* Take actual class notes while
still doodling in this book

* Join the X-men

* Become a pick-pocket

You know, Chelsea,
I'd really like to
keep some dignity.

Hey, I have
personal letters
signed by the
president —
I can make some
serious cash!

I can't draw
the legs.

ENGLISH NOTES:

Limerick: definition — a poem of five anapestic lines with the rhyme scheme AABBA. Second lowest form of literature, just above the screenplay.

ex: Man from Nantucket, There Once Was A (see handout)

There was a young woman named Jones,
Who pegged accusations like stones.
    She said, "The beauty of bullshit,
    Is that you can pull shit
That normally no one condones."

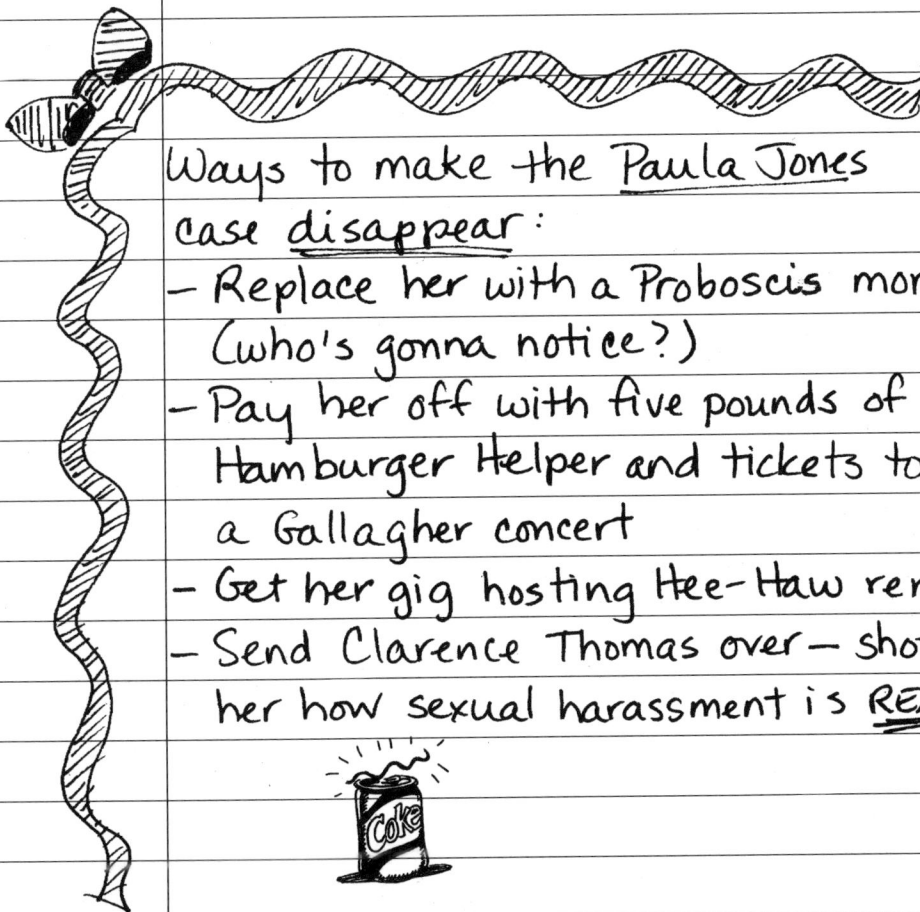

Ways to make the <u>Paula Jones</u> case <u>disappear</u>:
- Replace her with a Proboscis monkey (who's gonna notice?)
- Pay her off with five pounds of Hamburger Helper and tickets to a Gallagher concert
- Get her gig hosting Hee-Haw reruns.
- Send Clarence Thomas over — show her how sexual harassment is <u>REALLY</u> done.

"I'm a dancing queen!"

see that guy over there?

<u>What guy</u>?

THAT guy.

That guy

NO! THAT guy!

That's a girl.

Sorry, I messed up.
That guy!

Ok, so...

He's cute!

Full background check?

By tonight!

Coke

MAD MAX'S CRAZY FAXES

$$$ A BUCK A FAX, INCLUDING TAX! $$$

TO: ~~Dad~~ Chelsea

FROM: ~~chelsea~~ Dad

DATE: 10/17/97

TIME:

PAGES:)

(INCLUDING COVER)

COMMENTS: Dad, I'm thinking this is a good way to pick up some quick pocket money.

BUY <u>REAL</u> FBI FILES!

Need a little more leverage when asking a professor for that grad school rec?

Want the name and number of that person across the Quad who strips by their window?

Roommate secretly using your milk?

THE TRUTH <u>IS</u> OUT THERE! ONLY $200!!

Purchase two files, get a celebrity file of <u>your</u> choosing ABSOLUTELY FREE!

What do you think? ABSOLUTELY <u>NOT</u>!

Picasso (1881-1974)

- Cubism (orig. 1907) — style in which grains of reality dimly perceived within mishmash of abstract images. Foundation for modern political speech.
  - when viewed thru special 3-D glasses, paintings reveal dirty jokes (ha, ha!)

← No, just taking notes, see?

HEY, YOU'RE CHELSEA, RIGHT?.

RIGHT?.

Yes.

SO YOU'RE BIG STUFF, HUH?

OH, LIKE I DON'T TAKE NOTES?? LIKE YOU'RE A CLINTON, A PRESIDENT'S DAUGHTER SO YOU'RE SMART & YOU JUST SIT THERE SO SPECIAL THINKING HOW YOU'D NEVER GO OUT WITH A GUY FROM NEBRASKA AND SO WHAT IF I HAD CRABS IN THE 11TH GRADE, IT WENT AWAY AND LOTS OF PEOPLE GET CRABS 'CAUSE TH

Thanks, Tony.

I THINK YOU BROKE MY HAND

I'm like the Little Mermaid...
no, wait ... wait...
I'm a curly Pocahontas!

Mom's cookie recipe failed miserabl[y]
Maybe **I** can help jazz up the
White House image:

Pay off library fines —
Sell TV pilot ideas

He's a Russian Secret agent
She's the President's daughter
They're roommates !!
WACKINESS ensues !!!

CHATTING WITH CHELSEA
talk show
- PLUS: Come from white trash
        I know these people

THE CHELSEA CLINTON
MARGARITA
¼ cup fresh Lime juice
     (3-4 limes)
¼ cup Tequila
¼ cup Triple Sec
A handful of ice
1 cup TLC (TENDER
                LOVIN'
Cheers!   CHELSEA!)

CHELSEA **MORNINGS**
CHELSEA **NIGHTS**:

Student by day,
Astronaut by night
- Wackiness or weightlessness ensues

ROGER AND ME:
Uncle Rog and I go
sleuthing around U.S. in
Mystery Van.
- Budget bonus: Rog will
  work for food.

Zoiks, Scoob!

VRMMMM!!!

Chelsea ~~Depp~~
Chelsea ~~Pitt~~
Chelsea ~~Cruise~~
Chelsea ~~Duchovny~~
Chelsea ~~Reeves~~

Johnny Clinton
Brad Clinton
Tom Clinton
David Clinton
Keanu Clinton

Chelsea! Do you
[wan]t a Starburst?

Sure. Thanks!

[St]rawberry, right?

How did you
know that?

From the Internet.
My name's Lester!
I run the Chelsea Fan Club
web site. we've been hit 4,369
times this year, Chelsea.

[I]'m really not
hungry.

No Starburst? How about broccoli & cheese?
& cheese? I Know you like that.
I've got some in my pocket.

Tell-tale signs of my parents' Empty Nest Syndrome:
• Parents tried to adopt Janet Reno!
• Dad has started to develop a <u>concrete</u>
  foreign policy.
• Mom wanders around White House all day,
  burping the log cradled in her arms.
★ During State of the Union address, Dad sang
  "<u>Hush Little Baby</u>"

Ways to use my 1st Daughter Power for **good** rather than evil:

- Find out who in America buys Yanni records. Have them killed.
- Find out who in America buys Streisand records. Have them killed.
- Have Streisand killed. Frame Yanni. Have him sent to Turkish Prison.

Ways to use my 1st Daughter power for **evil** rather than good:

- Give Congressional Medal of Honor to Keifer Sutherland
- Get Adam Curry back on MTV
- Let Streisand live

My Dad messed with Texas... and kicked ass!

RUSH FEEDS THE HOMELESS

B.B.Q. SAUCE

American History   Prof. Schmaltz

Sharecropping (orig. 1865)
- plantation owners' rental
  of land and equipment
  ("40 acres and a mule")
  to former slave for
  % of crop

1   5   Q   2   _   A

Deals suggested before 40 Acres and a Mule
- 7 acres and some envelopes
- 5 Hail Marys and a rickshaw driver
- A six-pack and tickets to a Lakers game
- Two turtle doves and a partridge in a pear tree

C'mon, what's the last # in the Nuclear Launch Code?

Sorry Johnny you lost.

C'mon...

Nope. I gave you a mustache, a bow tie and every thing!

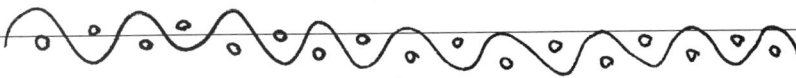

ANAGRAMS
for
President Clinton
Indecent Torn Slip
Decent Nostril Pin

BILL

BILL

SHREDDER 2000

Chelsea Clinton
Hell's Acne Tonie
Nice Clean Sloth
Leech Scant Loin

Mr. Veggie Magic
and his organic cornucopia
of vegetable merriment

FREE DELIVERY
MIN. CHARGE: A SMILE

Tel: (415) 514-LOVE

58 HAIGHT-ASHBURY
SAN FRANCISCO, CA

← Hey, isn't this people?

Luncheon Special

1. Merry Mashed Yeast and Plate of Alfalfa Sprouts $11.95
2. Chuckling Chick Peas in Happy Happy Sauce $8.25
3. Zany Zucchini in Wacky Wheatgrass Juice.................$8.75
4. Cinnamon $13.45
5. Veggie Lasagna (when the mood's upon ya) $2.25
6. Miraculous Tofu Monkey Brains...................................$9.85
7. Soylent Green...$4.25

And the Mr. Veggie Magic special

Mama Cass's Un-Ham Sandwich.................................$10.01

John 3:17 "And the Lord did say: feast upon these veggies whence sprang from my loins."

Buy 5 lbs of bean curd, get 1 garlic smoothee free!

TEST: How far will a felt-tipped pen's ink spread?

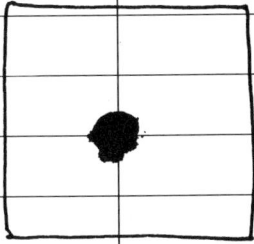
#1   :30 seconds

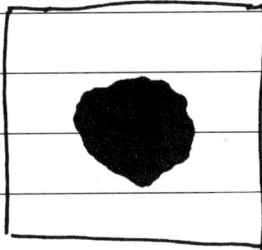
#2   1min, 30 sec

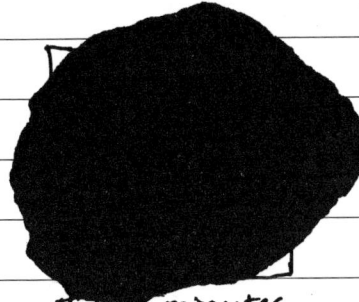
#3   15 minutes

ANTHRO 143

CHAPTER 3 — OUR PAST

- Prehuman ancestors varied in strength, appearance and intelligence. Some of fossilized remains are damaged and difficult to interpret, but scientists have been able to put the pieces of these puzzles together with great success.

- LANDMARK DISCOVERIES:

A. JAVA MAN, discovered by Dubois, had a small cranial capacity and bony ridges on skull.

B. NO JAW MAN, found in southern France, had no lower teeth and probably could not speak. Carbon dating indicates a penchant for the banjo.

Muffle voice, call Tipper, and mock her value systems

AIR FORCE ONE — CHOICE OF PRESIDENTS

ECONOMY CLASS

	CARRIER	FLT NMBR	DEPARTURE / ARRIVAL		SEAT	MEAL
NONREF						
CLINTON / CHELSEA MS						
FROM LOS ANGELES	AF1	003	1455	1620	WNDW SEAT	VGTRN / KSHR
TO AREA 51	UFO	***	2500	2500	SSPND ANMTN	XXXXVOIDXXXX
TO XXXXVOIDXXXX	AF1	004	1620	1735	ISLE SEAT	XXXXVOIDXXXX
TO WASHINGTON			XXXXVOIDXXXX		XXXXVOIDXXXX	XXXXVOIDXXXX

DINER'S CLUB BB KD VGG JT GB YDJT CODE: CALIF DREAMER

NON-SMOKING INFLIGHT MOVIE: TEEN WOLF 2: STARRING JASON BATEMAN SPECIAL REQUEST: XXXXVOIDXXXX

NON-HAIRCUT

0 09987 94556377 40   8896477362996748

TAKE ME
TO YOUR
FATHER!

<u>Other Areas Besides 51</u>
Area 71 — Congressional **Nude** Ranch
Area 16 — Rotisserie baseball field
Area 28 — "Lost" Tribe of Israel
Area 92 — My dorm room   olé!
Area 11 — Casa del Bogeyman
Area 3 — Tribunal of the Talking Pigs

YUM YUM YUM YUM

Grant Wood (1892-1947)

- His American folk style
  at first appears to be
  puckishly naïve, but
  upon further inspection
  reveals itself to be
  simplistic and infantile.

Chelsea

Chachi

Hierarchy of Art

Nude people (but no pull-out)
Sculptures w/ **stumps**
            for extremities

Blurry stuff
Paintings w/ lots of blue
Dogs playing poker
Larry Flynt publications
The œuvre of Yoko Ono !!!

The Ocean-floor Girls

Hey Chel, it's me! ☺
Can I have an M&M?
thanks!

Can I have an M&M?
thanks!

Can I have an M&M?
thanks!

Can I have an M&M?
No, a red one.

Get your OWN!

C. Everett Koop

FORMER SURGEON GENERAL

To Whom it May Concern,

Hello. My name is C. Everett Koop, you may recognize me from such administrations as President Reagan's and President Bush's. I am writing to assure you that Chelsea was, in fact, a very, very sick girl on December 2, when your History department administered an examination to the students of History 101, of which Chelsea is, and remains to be, a diligent and industrious student.

A horrible sickness it was indeed, ravaging poor Chelsea's fragile immune system, leaving her weak and incapacitated for a period of 24 hours, perhaps less. It's hard to tell because, being the valiant trooper that she is, young Chelsea, against the sagely advice of former Surgeon General C. Everett Koop (me), decided to go out and get some fresh air to aid her in her struggle against this vile malady.

It was there, at the Palo Alto Mall, that poor sickly Chelsea happened to see Professor Schmaltz. That Professor Schmaltz didn't take it upon himself to drive Chelsea home immediately shocks, and personally disturbs me. What kind of a "man" lets a 17-year-old girl, delirious with fever, walk around the Palo Alto Mall? Further, that he claims to have noticed no signs of fever or sickness in Chelsea strikes me as ludicrous. Take it from me, former Surgeon General C. Everett Koop, the sickly blue hue on Chelsea's mouth was not "from a slurpie" as Professor Schmaltz callously claims but the tell-tale signs of Chelsea's embattled immune system.

And before we cast aspersions upon this young innocent, let us cast into doubt the aspersion-caster himself. Was the Professor simply "pitching pennies into the wishing fountain," as he claimed, or was it something far more sinister? Perhaps he was "wishing" to be one of these nubile young mall-girls himself, prancing around in Catholic-school plaid miniskirts and knee-highs, giggling at cute boys and waiting to be impregnated. Pure conjecture? Perhaps. But who would you rather believe? Me, former Surgeon General C. Everett Koop or some freaky, Communist, cross-dressing professor?

Sincerely,

C. Everett Koop

C. Everett Koop
Former Surgeon General

Western Literature is based around certain core symbolic motifs: 1) Penis (P) 2) Jesus (J). Use these symbols to analyze the following poem.

The Second Coming – William Butler Yeats

Turning and turning in the widening gyre — P?
The falcon cannot hear the falconer; — Wings? Angel? Deaf angel? J??
Things fall apart; the centre cannot hold; — Made in USA
Mere anarchy is loosed upon the world,
The blood-dimmed tide is loosed, and everywhere
The ceremony of innocence is drowned;
The best lack all conviction, while the worst ⎤ — P (Remember "10-second Tommy" – Summer '96)
Are full of passionate intensity. ⎦

Surely some revelation is at hand; — Definitely P
Surely the Second Coming is at hand. — Ditto
The Second Coming! Hardly are those words out — obsess much?
When a vast image of *Spiritus* Mundi — post-coital guilt? / "you'll go blind"?? – J
Troubles my sight: somewhere in sands of the desert
A shape with lion body and the head of a man, | — Tipper. Ha ha.
A gaze blank and pitiless as the sun,
Is moving its slow thighs, whilt all about it
Reel shadows of the indignant desertbirds.
The darkness drops again; but now I know
That twenty centuries of stony sleep ⎤ — ask Uncle Rog… xx
Were vexed to nightmare by a rocking cradle.
And what rough beast, its hour come round at last,
Slouches towards Bethlehem to be born?

Remember: tell Dad to wear
bigger shorts on
his jogs

Note: withdraw application
to be baby-sitter for Kennedys

Johnny, what's up?
Bored yet?

No Way! I just
realized who Prof.
Schmaltz looks like.
Cover his beard with
your finger.

WHITES   DARKS   KEVLARS

Whoa, no wonder
he grades so hard!

Stupid printer isn't working again. NASA can kiss its Christmas bonus goodbye.

Chelsea

Socks

Thank-you cards for Xmas gifts

- The Gores (waffle iron)
- Free Masons (lock of Brad Pitt's hair)
- ★ Socks (dead mouse)
- Uncle Rog (2 oz Acapulco Gold)
- G.O.P. (Cliff notes to the Bible)
- Barbra Streisand
  (framed autographed photo of herself)
- Richard Gere (a jar of his tears)

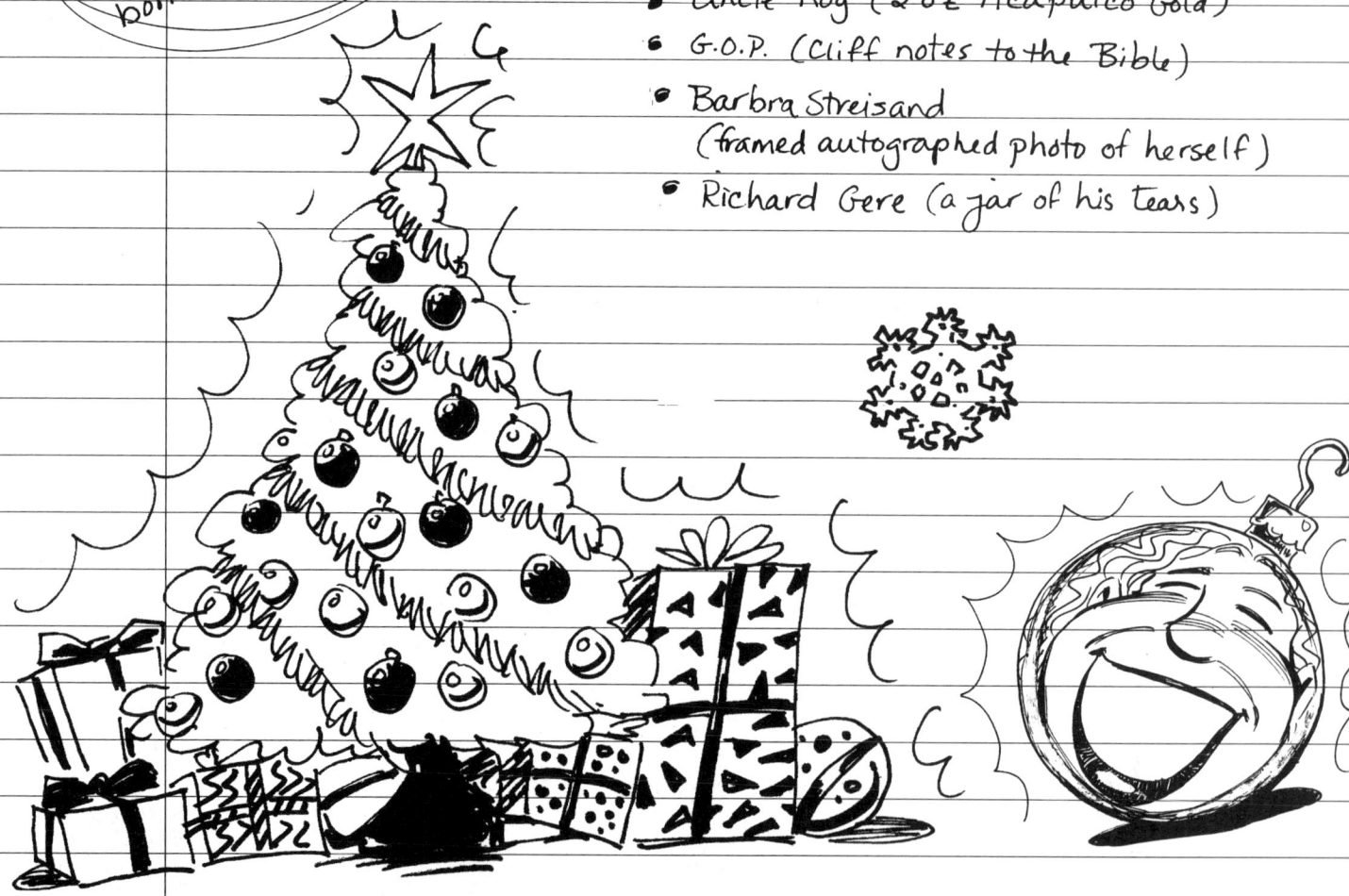

Tuesday Hung over. Skipped class. Get notes.

INVENTORY OF MY POCKET

PLAYBOY

680 N. Lakeshore Drive, CHICAGO, IL 60611

Dear Chelsea,

We are doing an issue dedicated to the Girls of the PAC-10. While we have already photographed many outstanding women (including this <u>great</u> piece of ass from Oregon!) your inclusion in this issue would add greatly to it. Playboy, as a cornerstone of taste and class, assures you that the pictorial would reflect our love of the Presidency. We made Patti Reagan a First Daughter Playmate that America could wave from majestic mountain tops and we'll do the same for you.

For this very special issue, we would place your pictorial between a very tasteful roundtable with Mickey Rourke and Noam Chomsky and a provocative article on the hot new carburetors of Detroit.

Imagine the marvel and delight of your parents when you present them with the images they have always cherished but could never fully recapture until now — you, Chelsea Clinton, just as you came into this God-fearing world, naked as a jaybird with riding crop in hand.

We have many ideas to share with you, all of which are quite tasteful. For instance, you on a tasteful Italian-leather saddle with a tasty ice cream cone. Perhaps something simpler like you wrapped up in an American flag, mostly. Certainly, we would be open to any creative input you may have.

Chelsea, we cannot and will not "exploit" your femininity or sense of dignity. Only you can do that. Remember, this is a celebration of the human form and the tasteful beauty of the female figure. Of course, we'll have to wait until you turn 18 to celebrate this stuff, but in the meantime please consider our offer.

We would be willing to pay $85,000 for a tasteful black and white pictorial, with an additional $15,000 bonus if you really show some skin.

Tastefully Yours,

The Heff

Yeesh! Patti Reagan...

Brad Pitt ROCKS!
Wait... I'm Chelsea,
I ROCK!

CHAP. 3 — (Review for exam!!!)

- **LANDMARK DISCOVERIES CONTINUED:**
  A. TABŪN WOMAN, unearthed in Israel in the first half of this century, had general Neanderthal features with a less pronounced forehead.

yadda yadda yadda

eww!

B. ARROW-LIKE PROTRUSION WOMAN, located by Miller, appeared to have a horn coming out of the right side of her head. May have been used for early, crude stand-up comedy routine.

Number of times Professor Pfaltzgraff said "um" this class:

LHT LHT LHT LHT
LHT LHT LHT LHT LHT
LHT LHT LHT LHT

TOTAL (77)

$$15 \times 5 \over 75$$
$$+3 \over 77$$

I'd rather be dancing!

THE CRANBERRIES

Biol. 101

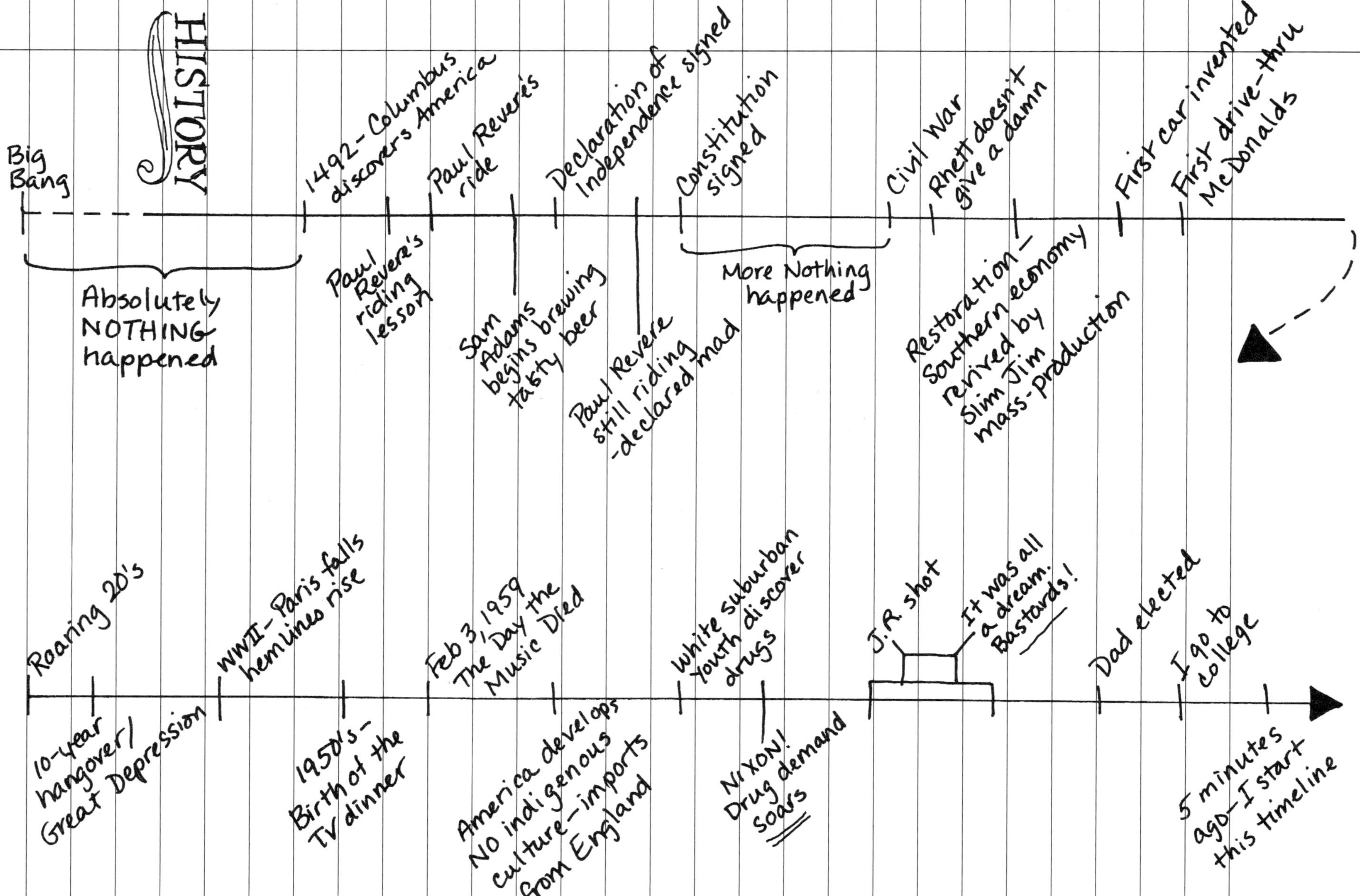
HISTORY
Big Bang
Absolutely NOTHING happened
1492 - Columbus discovers America
Paul Revere's riding lesson
Paul Revere's ride
Sam Adams begins brewing tasty beer
Declaration of Independence signed
Paul Revere still riding - declared mad
Constitution signed
More Nothing happened
Civil War
Rhett doesn't give a damn
Restoration - Southern economy revived by Slim Jim mass-production
First car invented
First drive-thru McDonalds
Roaring 20's
10-year hangover/ Great Depression
WWII - Paris falls hemlines rise
1950's - Birth of the TV dinner
Feb 3, 1959 The Day the Music Died
America develops NO indigenous culture - imports from England
White suburban youth discover drugs
NIXON! Drug demand soars
J.R. shot
It was all a dream. Bastards!
Dad elected
I go to college
5 minutes ago - I start this timeline

yee-haaaa!

General Lee

BRUMMM!!

HISTORY NOTES

I AM C.C. RIDER!

Henry Ford — considered mad by his partners when he dreamed of making 1,000 cars a day

— later <u>proven</u> mad when he wanted to run them on liquid cheese

1913 — invention of assembly-line; revolutionized all industry

— paved way for that wacky, classic "**I Love Lucy**" episode in the chocolate factory

♫ I'm just a Bill ♪

Pope-mobile

PUT PUT

Bicycle-built-for-five

"Low-ri-der..." ♪♫

RMM!

El Camino with
El Salvadoran Death Squad

Hi! I'm Tony. I'm a bodyguard. Many people think that bodyguards lead **boring** lives, but I do a lot of really neat things. Why, just look at my scintillating day:

5:45 AM — Wake up. Smile. With ~~that~~ out of the way, greet Mr. Sun with a serious nod.

6:00 AM — Eat very serious breakfast (bran muffins, sugar-free cereal, coffee taken black, more bran muffins).

6:17 AM — Meditate on how much I like Chelsea.

7:20 AM — Read Wall Street Journal (above the fold) during very serious bowel movement.

8:03 AM — Groove out to swingin' sounds of Karen Carpenter

8:07 AM — Easy there, Tiger! Cool down.

9:00 AM — Believe in love.

9:58 AM — Practice motion of putting finger to ear in very serious manner.

10:15 AM — Think, again, of just whom I am trying to impress.

12:00 PM — Don Ray-Bans. Try acting cool.

5:02 PM — Fail miserably.

5:30 PM — Chelsea has dance class. I get to live out unspoken dreams.

7:30 PM — Ponder meaning of life.

7:47 PM — Reach conclusion. Organize money in wallet by serial number.

9:56 PM — Music blasting from Chelsea's room. How can one woman **be so cool**?

11:00 PM — Fitful sleep. Maintain state of cat-like awareness.

You know, this is my job.

Tony, I was joking. c'mon. Hello?

I'm not talking to you. You stink.

Won't you take a bullet for me anymore?

We'll see.

Fine. You win.

cool!

The Goregoyles

Jackie O's stuff went for bucks!

WHAT ABOUT **MY STUFF?**

Call Christies and Sotheby's ASAP!!

Items:

★ **Lot 209 — Backpack**
Used it to defend myself from Shiite terrorists who took advantage of my bodyguard Tony while tying his shoelace. Poor condition, slashed several times by those crazy curved swords (scimitars?). $400

★ **Lot 364 — Nightgown**
Reinforced Kevlar with pink lace. Worn only once. By Tony. Made obsolete by space-age silk teddie created by CIA. $725

★ **Lot 429 — Signed Lunch**
One slice of Stanford cafeteria pizza signed by me in permanent marker. Cheese and Pepperoni. Small bite off the tip, but otherwise in good condition. $320

★ **Lot 582 — Notebook**
↖ no one would pay money for this!

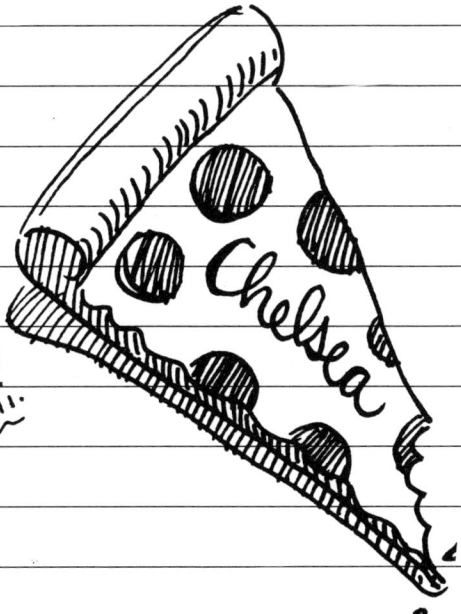

Chelsea

Happy B-day to me

HAPPY BIRTHDAY CHELSEA!!

Feb. 27th
18!!
Finally able to vote!
Tell Mom she has my vote in **2000**!

PARTY!

Happy Birthday Chelsea.

thanks, Johnny! Can I take you out for a birthday dinner?

YES! I would really love to —

I'll need your Social Security Number, son.

Tony, stay OUT of this!

A PONY!!

Dear Uncle Al,

   Thank you for the care package. You've been so nice. Al, don't you believe those reports in the media about you having "as much charm as a cardboard television." You're ~~nice~~ ~~full of energy~~ ~~actually quite exciting~~ wonderful. Sure, on the outside you don't seem to have much charisma, personality, sense of humor, or good taste in wives. But I know (and I think you know it, too) that somewhere on the inside, where no one can really see it, buried deep down, somewhere a couple of inches to the left of the pancreas, you've got ~~talent~~ ~~real je ne sais quoi~~ it.

   By the way, I saw ~~the CNN footage of~~ you at the state funeral for the Minister of Cattle Insemination in ~~Liberia~~ Latvia. I understand your trying to spice up your image and I understand it was reasonably fair-weathered, but hot-pants ~~were repulsive~~ really don't suit you.

   Al, I know things are tough for you right now, so I'll sign off by saying: when the phone records are against you and bad press is all about you, when the Buddhist nuns are subpoenaed and your future looks in doubt, well then Al, you get out there and give it all you got and win just one for the Tipper.

The Big Dipper and the Big Tipper

Dance Steps I Have Learned

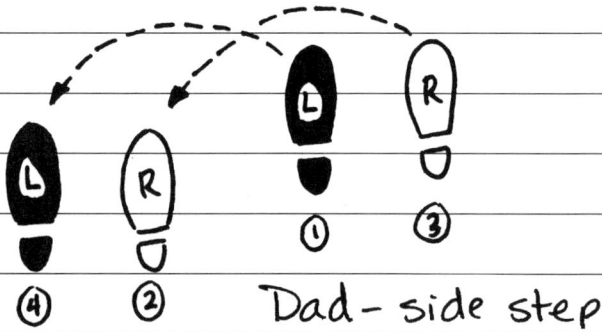

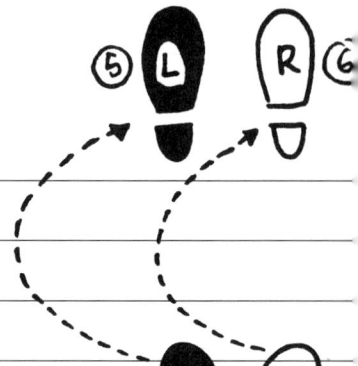

Dad - side step

Newt - Goose step

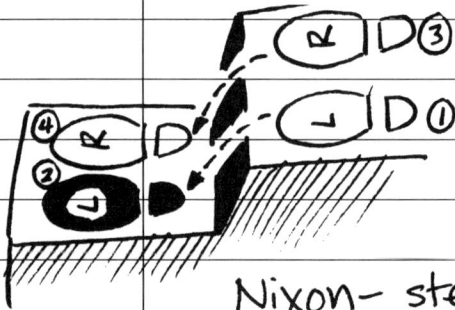

(CLICK HEELS)

Nixon - step down

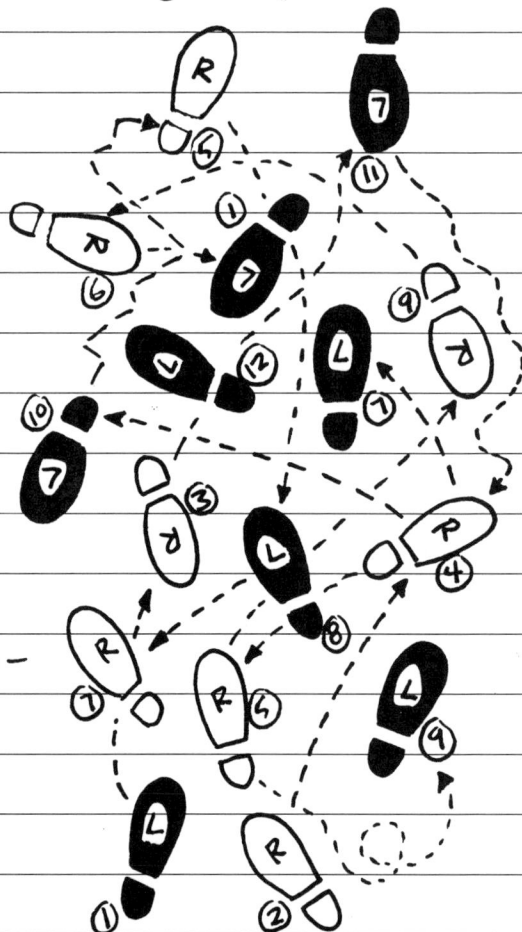

Kitty
Dukakis -
12 step

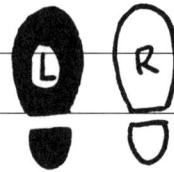

20th CENTURY

Jesse Helms - out of step

Yum!

Possible <u>Tattoos</u>!
- Anchor on forearm (like Tony)
- Tipper's "*Parental Advisory*" warning on <u>inner thigh</u>
- Gorbachev's birthmark (placement?)
- Swiss acct. #0-8739-6, password: Giblet
- Daisy chain around ankle (blend in with <u>every</u> <u>other</u> <u>college</u> <u>woman</u>)

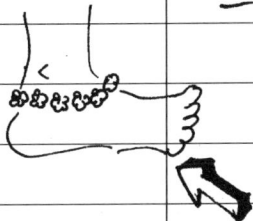

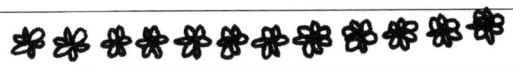

Tony, could you go out and get me some condoms?

What's this word?

Condoms.

Forget it. No way. Absolutely Not.

It <u>is</u> the nineties.

This deal just keeps getting worse and worse

Me in Swan Lake!

DANCE!

NUCLEAR SQUIRREL
1500 Series

SPECIFICS
HEIGHT AT FULL ARM/LEG EXTENSION = 14.32 INCHES
LENGTH WITH FULL TAIL EXTENTION (SQUIRREL UPRIGHT) = 15.95 INCHES
WIDTH (ARMS AT FULL EXTENTION) = 10.84 INCHES
WEIGHT (EXCLUDING CHESTNUT) FIRST AID POUCH LOADED = 8.04LBS
MAXIMUM LAND SPEED FULLY LOADED = 46.5 MPH
MAXIMUM VERTICAL CLIMB SPEED FULLY LOADED = 72.2 MPH
MAXIMUM COMPRESSIVE PRESSURE OF HYDRAULIC HANDS = 3200 PSI
MAXIMUM LEAP DISTANCE (LEVEL SURFACE) = APX. 1250 FT
VOLUME OF TAIL AT FULL INFLATION = 6000 CUBIC INCHES

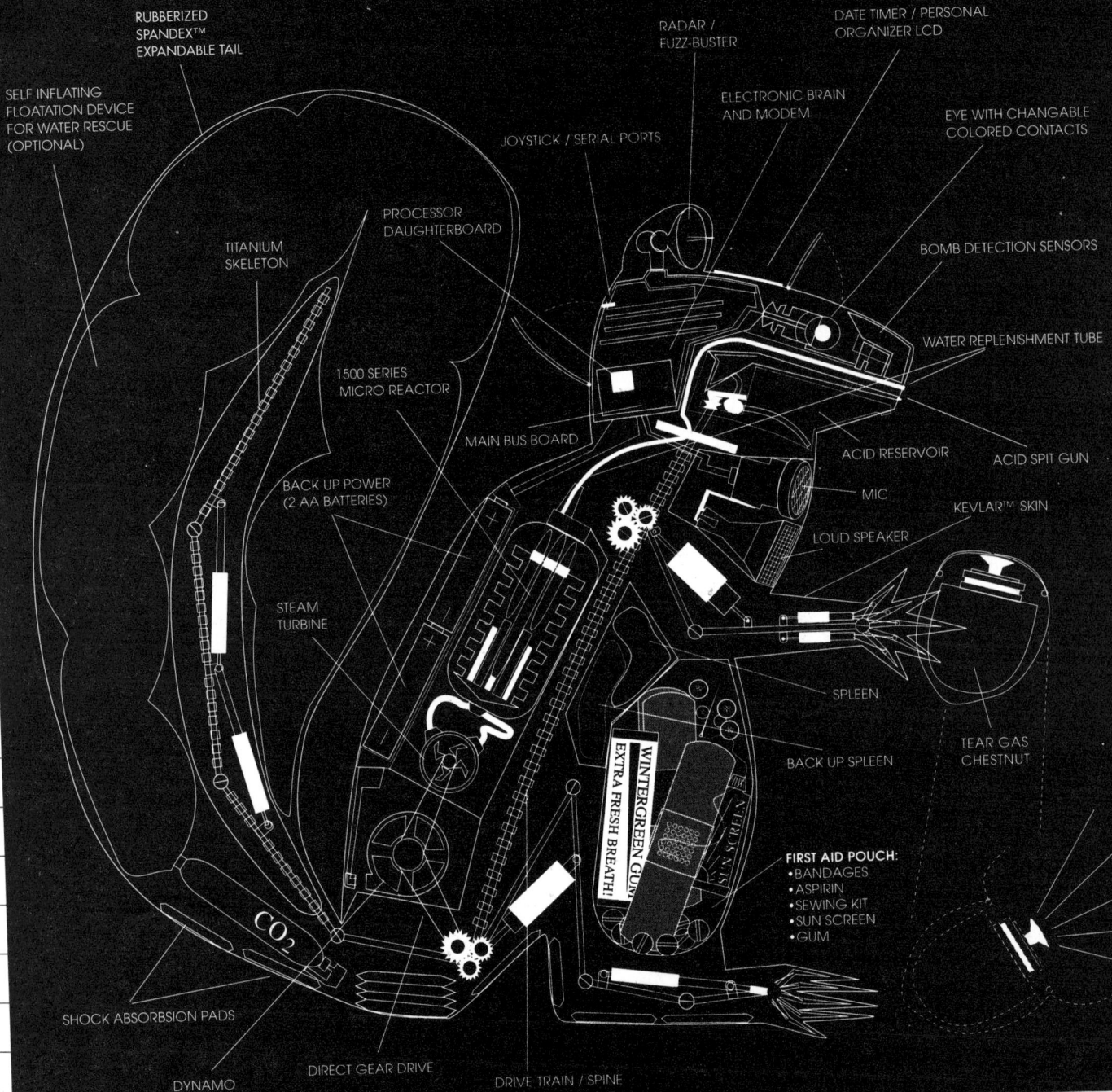

RUBBERIZED SPANDEX™ EXPANDABLE TAIL

SELF INFLATING FLOATATION DEVICE FOR WATER RESCUE (OPTIONAL)

RADAR / FUZZ-BUSTER

DATE TIMER / PERSONAL ORGANIZER LCD

ELECTRONIC BRAIN AND MODEM

EYE WITH CHANGABLE COLORED CONTACTS

JOYSTICK / SERIAL PORTS

PROCESSOR DAUGHTERBOARD

TITANIUM SKELETON

BOMB DETECTION SENSORS

WATER REPLENISHMENT TUBE

1500 SERIES MICRO REACTOR

MAIN BUS BOARD

ACID RESERVOIR

ACID SPIT GUN

BACK UP POWER (2 AA BATTERIES)

MIC

KEVLAR™ SKIN

STEAM TURBINE

LOUD SPEAKER

SPLEEN

BACK UP SPLEEN

TEAR GAS CHESTNUT

WINTERGREEN GUM
EXTRA FRESH BREATH!

SUN SCREEN

FIRST AID POUCH:
• BANDAGES
• ASPIRIN
• SEWING KIT
• SUN SCREEN
• GUM

CO_2

SHOCK ABSORBSION PADS

DYNAMO

DIRECT GEAR DRIVE

DRIVE TRAIN / SPINE

THE 1500 SERIES **NSQ** REPRESENTS THE NEXT GENERATION NBPS (NATURE BASED PROTECTION SYSTEM). EXPANDING AND UPGRADING THE BEST FEATURES OF THE 700 SERIES, AND REDESIGNING OR ELIMINATING PROBLEMATIC SYSTEMS, THE NEW NSQ ACHIEVES A RELIABILTY AND DESTRUCTIVE FORCE NEVER BEFORE POSSIBLE. SIGNIFICANT IMPROVEMENTS INCLUDE: A REDESIGNED FIRST AID KIT 12% LARGER THAN THE PREVIOUS MODEL UTILIZING A VELCRO™ STRIP INSTEAD OF THE RATHER CLUMSY ZIPPER, AND EMPLOYING THE NEW "OUCHLESS" BAND-AID, ENHANCED SPEAKER FIDELITY AND VOLUME WHICH MAY NOW BE ADJUSTED EASILY (WITHOUT EVER TOUCHING A SCREWDRIVER) WITH OUR NEW SQUIRRELSOUND™ SOFTWARE (INCLUDED), A LARGER LCD FOR THE PERSONAL ORGANIZER AND INCREASED MEMORY CAPACITY ALLOWING FOR OVER 6500 INDIVIDUAL ENTRIES AND NOTES, AND NEW SOFTWARE DESIGNED TO REDUCE THE 700 SERIES' PROPENSITY TO BURN AND DECAPITATE SMALL BIRDS. ALL SQUIRREL PARTS ARE MADE IN THE USA. TEAR GAS CHESTNUT (CONSTRUCTED OF HIGH DENSITY CERAMICS WITH MAHOGANY INLAYS) IS NOW MADE IN JAPAN.

Johnny ♥

Tony, my date's tonight. Can you call in sick or injured?

Sorry. No can do.

How about I accidentally hit you in the head with a crowbar?

Nuclear Squirrel gone bad

Nope.

I could shoot you. Claim you took a bullet for me.

Look, I'm just as unhappy having to watch 2 freshmen on a 1st date, but it's me or the Nuclear Squirrel!

Animals I can make with letters in my name:

seal   leech
lion   cat
ant   sea lion

Nuclear Squirrel?

Take a look.

FINE.

SPONTANEOUS ROMANTIC WALK PLAN

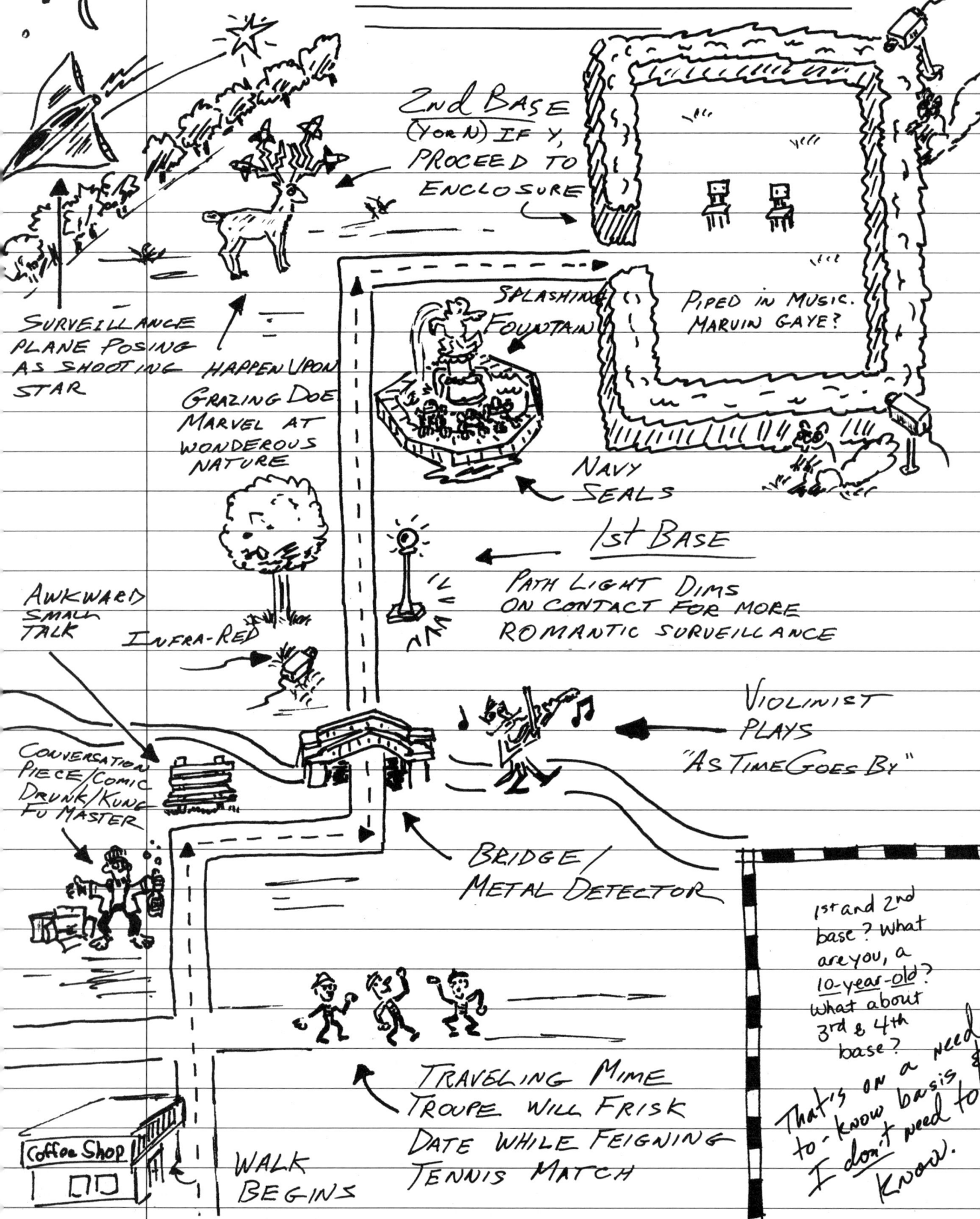

2nd BASE (Y or N) IF Y, PROCEED TO ENCLOSURE

PIPED IN MUSIC. MARVIN GAYE?

SURVEILLANCE PLANE POSING AS SHOOTING STAR

HAPPEN UPON GRAZING DOE MARVEL AT WONDEROUS NATURE

SPLASHING FOUNTAIN

NAVY SEALS

1st BASE

PATH LIGHT DIMS ON CONTACT FOR MORE ROMANTIC SURVEILLANCE

AWKWARD SMALL TALK

INFRA-RED

VIOLINIST PLAYS "AS TIME GOES BY"

CONVERSATION PIECE/COMIC DRUNK/KUNG FU MASTER

BRIDGE/ METAL DETECTOR

1st and 2nd base? what are you, a 10-year-old? what about 3rd & 4th base? That's on a need-to-know basis & I don't need to know.

Coffee Shop

WALK BEGINS

TRAVELING MIME TROUPE WILL FRISK DATE WHILE FEIGNING TENNIS MATCH

Sorry about last night

Yeah, I have a great date and you go and break his nose! Some body guard.

Away from prying eyes of Washington, possible memoir for west-coast publisher.

Some possible chapters:

Chp. 1 — The Presidential Family: A womb's-eye view
Chp. 2 — An Arkansas Adolescence: Coping with an IQ above 30
Chp. 3 — Newt Stalkings
Chp. 4 — White House Tragedy: How I accidentally saw Al Gore in his tighty-whities
Chp 5 — The Gore-Gore Girls: blonde hair, dark roots, dark souls

I said I was sorry.

I really am sorry.

Whatever.

HAHAHAHAHAHAHAHAHAHAH

Note: Way to thank SNL for hilariously intelligent and mature skit about me: Force Lorne Michaels to make high-budget sequel to "It's Pat: The Movie".

HOUSE OF THYESTES   HOUSE OF ATREUS

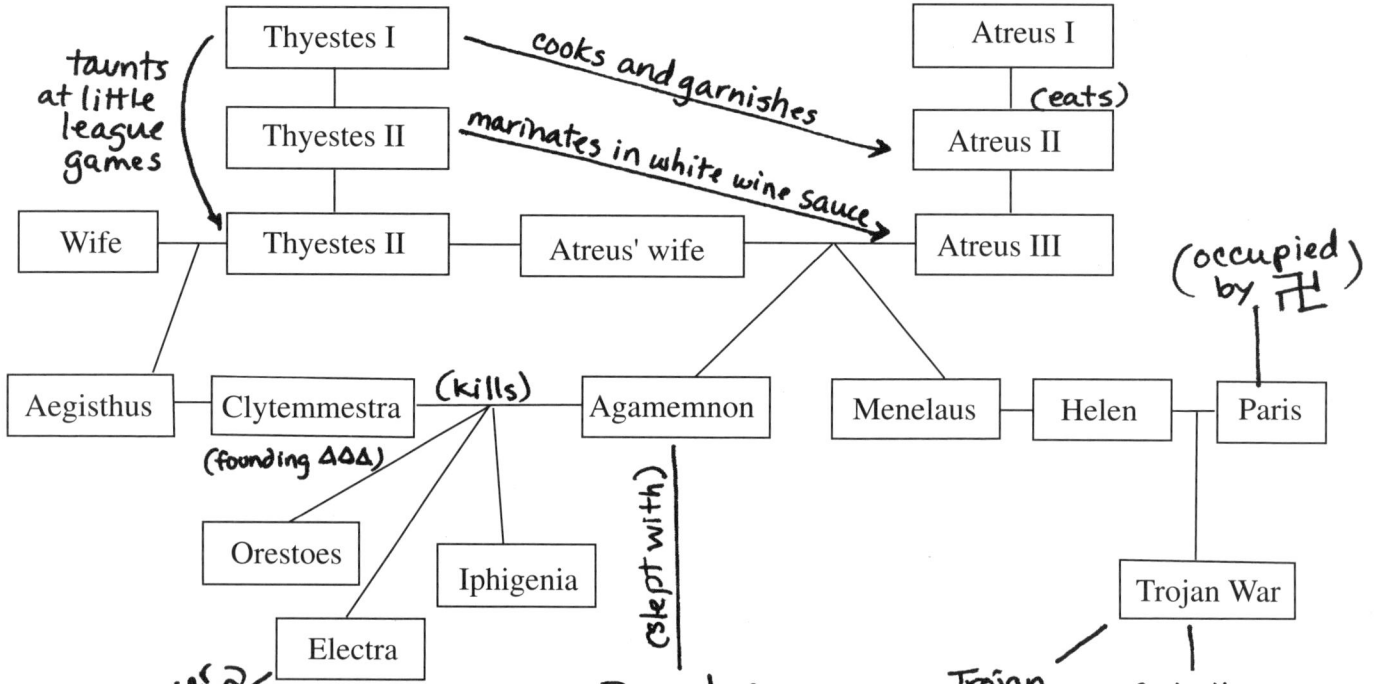

taunts at little league games

Thyestes I —— cooks and garnishes ——> Atreus I

Thyestes II —— marinates in white wine sauce ——> Atreus II (eats)

Wife —— Thyestes II —— Atreus' wife —— Atreus III

(occupied by 卍)

Aegisthus —— Clytemmestra —— (kills) —— Agamemnon   Menelaus —— Helen —— Paris

(founding ΔΘΔ)

Orestoes   Iphigenia

Electra

(slept with)

(nuttier than)   (nutty as)

(hooked up with) Brandon   (sibling)   Trojan Horse (slept with)   Achilles (kills)

HOUSE OF SPELLING

Fruitcake   Kelly   Brenda   Mr. Clean   Ajax

(slept with) Dylan   (slept with)   (slept with)   (slept with)

(nuttier than) Oedipus

Starred with Paul Reubens in Buffy the Vampire Slayer   Ivory Soap Girl

Christmas Dinner

Starred with Danny DeVito in Batman Returns   Starred in Rabid directed by David Cronenberg

Christmas Ham

Starred with Jack Nicholson in Hoffa   Cronenberg directed The Fly with Jeff Goldblum

Nicholson in A Few Good Men with

Pig —— (back to) ——>

Goldblum starred in Big Chill with Kevin Costner

KEVIN BACON!   <—— (back to) —— Costner in JFK with

"NO, Mr. Gingrich, I expect you to die."

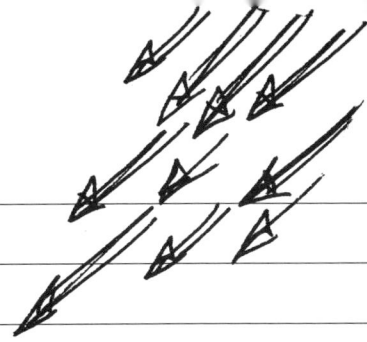

Tony — find who pulled that fire alarm at 4 a.m. Have his legs broken.

HISTORY

Paper Topics

Communism: Can Two Billion Chinese Really be Wrong?

Mustard Gas & Pepper Spray: Condiments of Evil?

Bob Hope: The Enemy Within?

Guilty! If O.J. Had Been Tried in the 40's

The 50's: Our Boring World Before Crack

The Great Depression: Would Prozac Have Helped?

WWII: Did We Open Up a Can of Whoop-ass or What?!

THE LETTER OF ST. JUDE

To whom it may concern:

You now hold the secret of unending happiness and the means of your own destruction. Make twenty copies of this letter and pass them on to your friends. If you do this, truest luck will follow where ever you may go. This good fortune may take the form of good health, cash prizes, or possibly even meaningless sex. Do not follow these instructions, and your total ruin may be at hand. <u>THIS IS NOT A HOAX!</u>

Take for instance the story of Ignis Holland, a poor Idaho potato farmer whose wife had left him for a producer of squash. Well aware he could hardly compete with the romantic, high-society life style of squash farming, Ignis had given up hope of her return. As if that wasn't enough, his potato crop was suffering badly from a strange variety of head lice.

It was at this time that he received the letter of St. Jude. Being a God fearing man, he passed it along to twenty of his friends suggesting earnestly that they do the same. Within three days his crop began to flourish enabling him to sign a lucrative contract with a major fast food chain. One day later, Ignis's wife returned after the squash farmer was killed in a gruesome polo accident. They now live together in an enormous mansion made of a stucco-like compound produced from the carcasses of a billion lice.

Renee Applegate was not so lucky. In 1993, the wealthy young lady graduated at the top of her business school class and soon took a cushy job managing a large mutual fund. It was at this time she received a copy of this letter. Ms. Applegate, not believing in anything she could not understand on a balance sheet, ignored the letter and threw it in the trash. One week later while asleep her California home, she was kidnapped by Indonesian slave traders and taken out of the country against her will. On a small island in the Gulf of Thailand, she was sold to a powerful military officer from Burma. For two years she was his slave, until she escaped in a truck filled with rotting water buffalo meat. She was somehow able to procure a flight to South Africa, hoping that from there she could make it home. But her plane never arrived in Jonestown. A violent storm ripping through the Indian Ocean sent her plane crashing down in the remotest regions of Madagascar. There, bruised and broken, she emerged from the wreckage only to be devoured by a strange variety of carnivorous lemur.

Follow the instructions of this letter -- or do not. The choice is yours. The consequences are yours as well.

Send to:

Rush
Trent Lott
Mary Matalin

Sonny Bono
Ralph Reed
Prof. Schmaltz
etc.

Signed,

A Well-Wisher

DO NOT IGNORE THIS LETTER!

Art History   Prof. Decré

Pop Art — American movement of the 50's and 60's
           celebrates "common" culture

           Warhol (1928 – 1987) – Repeated image, interest in
                                   mass-production
                                 – Studio/drug den called
                                   "The Factory"

                                 – Used underage migrant
                                   workers in sweatshop
                                   conditions to "paint" "his"
                                   "masterpieces"
                                     –Inspired Kathie Lee (REGIS RULES!)

                                 – Pioneered concept of artist
                                   dying really, really rich, and
                                   not really being an artist

                                          ← REALLY
                                            EXPENSIVE

Lichtenstein (1923 – 1997) – BIG comic books

Darn!
Keanu's at the
door, and I
burned the
meat loaf!

If they build a
town in my honor,
I hope there's a
giant steel
abstract likeness
of me next to the
courthouse or
something.

I'm thinking of getting a plant for my room. Or an electric fence. Either way it'll liven things up a bit.

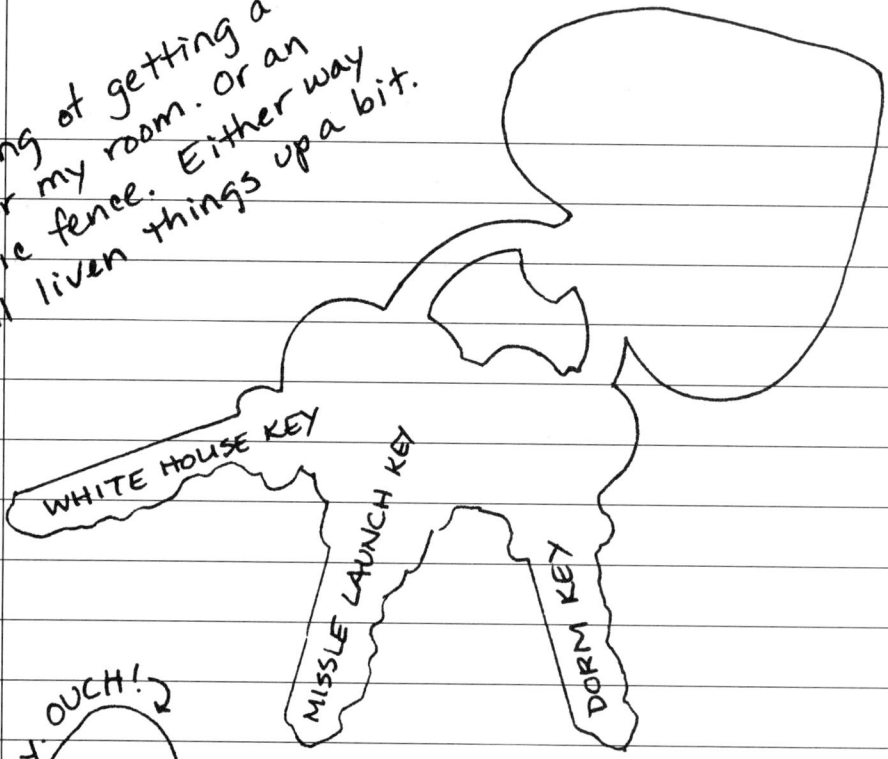

WHITE HOUSE KEY

MISSLE LAUNCH KEY

DORM KEY

Get me NODOZ!!!

what's this word?

NO DOZ!!! ARE YOU BLIND?

I bought you a box la Night.

SO? SO? you wanna make something of it JACK?

It's Tony

Broke this nail yesterday. OUCH!

Finger!

Finger!

Finger!

My hand!

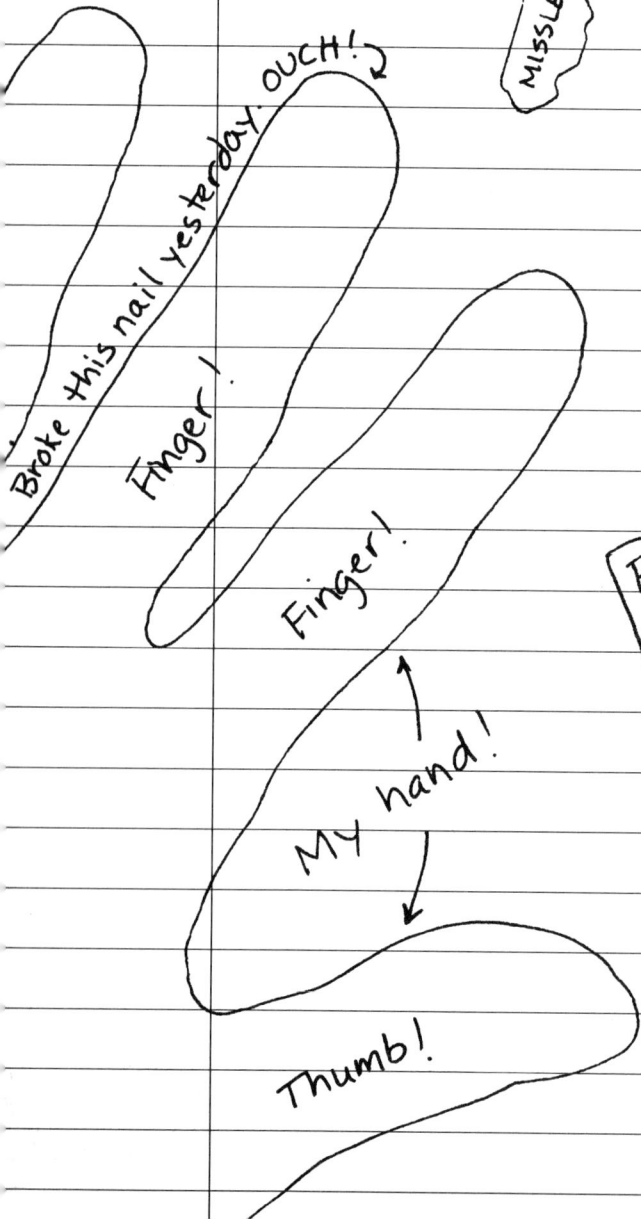

Boy, I'd be in all the papers if I SHOT somebody!

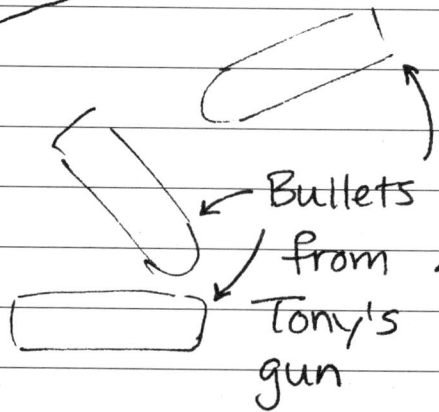

Thumb!

Bullets from Tony's gun

I want those Back.

No-Doz days & sleepless nights

I am the Lizard King !!

CAFFEINE   NO-DOZE!
              NO-DOZE

mma had a baby and her head popped off

JOLT!

I am the Eggman

I'm about to lose control and
I think I Like it !!

President's daughter President's daughter President's daughter
Worrying about the cameras and press and parents.
Worrying. about the
Worrying. I wish I were an ant—just the littlest thing.
I wouldn't have to think about the **press** or the **aliens**
or solving world crises, or anything. I could just

be **me**. A girl who skipped through third grade and danced her way to college.

I want to **CURSE AT THE TOP OF MY LUNGS!!!**
I want to get **WASTED.**
I want to drive off a cliff.....
I want to run in circles
   till I'm so dizzy I fall down!

I just want to be alone.
I wish I were an Oscar Meyer weiner.

All work and no play makes Chelsea a dull girl. All work and no play makes Chelsea a dull girl. All work and no play makes Chelsea a dull girl. All work and no play makes Chelsea a dull girl. All work and no play makes Chelsea a dull girl. All work and no play makes Chelsea a dull girl. All work and no play makes Chelsea a dull girl. All work and no play makes Chelsea a dull girl. All work and no play makes Chelsea a dull girl. All work and no play makes Chelsea a dull girl. All work and no play makes Chelsea a dull girl. All work and no play makes Chelsea a dull girl. All work and no play makes Chelsea a DULL GIRL!!! All work and no play makes Chelsea a dull girl! All work and no play makes Chelsea a **dull girl**! **All work and no play makes Chelsea a dull girl!!!** All work and no play makes Chelsea a dull girl. All work and no play makes Chelsea a dull girl. All work and no play makes Chelsea a dull girl. All work and no play makes Chelsea a dull girl. All work and no play make Chelsea a dull girl. All work and no play makes Chelsea a dull Girl. All work and no play makes Chelsea a **dull girl**. All work and no play makes Chelsea a dull girl. All work and no play makes Chelsea a dull girl. All work and no play makes Chelsea a dull girl. All work and no play makes Chelsea a dull girl. All work and no play makes

Chelsea a dull girl. All work and no play makes Chelsea a dull girl. All work and no play makes Chelsea a dull girls. All work and no play makes Chelsea a dull girl. All work and no play makes Chelsea a dull girl. All work and no play makes Chelsea a dull girl. All work and no play makes Chelsea a dull girl. All work and no play makes Chelsea a dull girl. All work and no play makes Chelsea a dull girl. ALL WORK AND NO PLAY MAKES CHELSEA A DULL GIRL. ALL WORK AND NO PLAY MAKES CHELSEA A DULL GIRL. ALL WORK AND NO PLAY MAKES CHELSEA A DULL GIRL. ALL WORK AND NO PLAY MAKES CHELSEA A DULL GIRL. ALL WORK AND NO PLAY MAKES CHELSEA A DULL GIRL. ALL WORK AND NO PLAY makes CHELSEA a DULL girl. All work and no play makes Chelsea a dull girl. All work and no play makes Chelsea a dull girl. All work and no play makes Chelsea a dull girl. all work and no play makes Chelsea a dull girl. All work and no play makes Chelsea a dull girl. All work and NO PLAY makes Chelsea a DULL GIRL! ALL WORK AND NO PLAY MAKES CHELSEA A DULL GIRL!!! All work and no play makes Chelsea a dull girl. All work and no play makes Chelsea a dull girl. All work and no play makes Chelsea a dull girl. All work and no play makes Chelsea a dull girl.

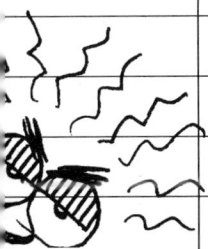

WHITE HOUSE

OFFICIAL FACSIMILE TRANSMISSION

TO: Chelsea

DATE:

TIME: 2:14 AM

FROM: Dad

PAGES: 1

(INCLUDING COVER)

COMMENTS: I don't want to hear any more crazy ideas about transferring to Devry!

THE INFORMATION CONTAINED IN THIS MESSAGE IS CONFIDENTAL INFORMATION INTENDED ONLY FOR THE USE OF THE INDIVIDUAL OR ENTITY NAMED ABOVE. IF YOU HAVE RECEIVED THIS FACSIMILE IN ERROR, PLEASE VISIT YOUR NEARBY DMV AND SAY "TIMMY FOUND A TUBER." THEY WILL HAND YOU SOME BLUE PILLS. WRAP THE PILLS WITH THE PAGES OF THIS FACSIMILE. SWALLOW. DIE. THANK YOU.

Spring Break Ideas!!

- Check obituaries in sunny places.
  Attend state funeral.
- Juarez weekend w/Uncle Rog.
  Find out: what is a "cat house"?
- Land Presidential helicopter on
  MTV Beach House.
  Optional: on MTV VJ ← Dead VJ is funny!
- Freak out Secret Service —
  fake illness, save medication
  and throw BIG PARTY!
- Have gun, will travel!

Tony!
You got your stupid chocolate in my peanut butter!

Well you got your peanut butter in MY Chocolate!

Yeah, well... wait, this is pretty good!

Good? This is Great! Hey! Gimme back my peanut butter!

Fat chance.

Chelsea Clinton

English 101

Professor Gobang

4/25/98

Very Good!

Veni, Vidi, Fishi — I Came, I Saw, I Fished.
Symbolism and Symbolic Meaning in The Old Man and The Sea

The Old Man and the Sea, by Earnest
Hemingway, is a book filled with
symbolism. If broken down, nearly every
aspect of the book can be seen as a
symbol for something. These symbols play
an important role and come together to
build one of the most important books in
the english language, or even other
languages.

The most prevalent symbol in the
book is water. It's everywhere. Now,
traditional literatic theory tells us
that wherever there's water, there's the
Baptism Motif. And an old Chinese proverb
tells us that where there's smoke,
there's fire. Thus, we can conclude that
the sea, as illustrated by the water,
symbolizes the Baptism Motif.

Had the fortuitous Mr. Hemingway
written the book The Old Man and the Sea
as The Old Man and the Desert, a great
deal of symbolism would have been lost.

The whole fishing thing would have a lot less impact, for example. ✓

Old men usually symbolize decay, wretchedness, and gum disease, however they can sometimes be seen as a symbol for decay, *nobility* and gum disease. In this case, it is quite probably the latter.

why do you think so — Cite examples

Much like an actual fish, the symbolic meaning, or significance, of the literary fish is slippery and hard to grasp. Traditional literatic study tells us that the fish is a symbol for Christ, or a Christ-like figure, or a figure who really resembles a Christ-like figure a lot. What is Hemingway trying to tell us by including a fish in his *piece de resistance*, as the french would say, or *Magnum Opus*, as the Latins would say?

CAP *?*

I don't know. But one can take a pretty good guess.

TP? *What?*

However, the meaning could be far more simplistic. In the beginning, Santiago meets up with the boy. He asks the boy to buy him a beer. We are all familiar with the common expression "to drink like a fish." Is this whole book merely a cry for help; a plea, if you will, from a desperate and lonely old man on the verge of a bender?

Source (

What do you think?

SPLAT!

I don't know. And he killed himself, *OH.*
so I guess we never will. But it
certainly does make you think. *So True...*

Perhaps the fish is simply a
representation for the astrological
symbol Pisces, (February 18 to March 19; ✓
savvy in business, but unlucky in love).
But who would that particular person be?
Santiago? The boy? The author himself?
Certainly, a library open after 2 AM
would have helped ascertain the truth.

In conclusion, it must be stated
with all certainty, that the numerous
symbols serve to reinforce and bolster
the author's use of these very symbols
and allow for a novel which is chock full
of meaning. Sometimes the meaning is
apparent, as in the case of the sea.
Other times, it is shrouded in literary
✓ mumbo-jumbo, so that only research and
hard work give us a glimpse into this   *3-5*
strange and mystical world known as   *Pages?*
Earnest Oliver Hemingway. Who wrote The
Old Man and the Sea, of which this paper
is about.

Chelsea,
I don't understand most of this,
but you make some original observations
and I'm pretty sure you read the book.

A-
B+

```
                         BIKINI
                         E
                         TANNING
        W                C
        H                H
        I              CHELSEA
CORRUPT               A   S
   R        E    B     L      STUPID          M
   A        WASHINGTON        A  A            O
   C        S    A     F    O   U DECEPTION
   K      NEWT    BOYS      W    L            E
          L    E       R         A            Y
          L    R   SUNNY
       MOM            I         S
   S   U           AWESOME   WASTED
POLITICS           U    X    A       R
   E   S   P       R    S    R       U
   A       I       FREEDOM           G
   Z     NUTS      S    X    C       S
   E               U    SEX
                   P    A
                        N
```

Inform California:
This week's winning
Lotto number is:
274185

White House
Documents

History 101--Final Exam

Short Paragraphs. Discuss the various factors that
defined American military policy in the following
events. Be sure to use facts to support your answers.

CLASSIFIED
INFORMATION
BY ORDER OF CIA
IN CONCORDANCE WITH §HV7632-A

1: Cuban Missile Crisis: Unknown to the general population,
CIA files reveal that Castro has just unveiled his powerful,
giant ████████████████████ described as "missle-like" by
bystanders ████████████████████ Ann-Margaret. Castro
rejected the offer. ████████████████████ with Bardzini dead,
Hymen Roth and JFK attended ████████████████████ ✓
████████ Sept. 3rd, 1962 at the Copacabana ████████
████████ head lining Ricky Ricardo. This outrage prompted
JFK into action citing the greater good of American culture.
                    ← really?

2: Korean War:
Nov. 17, 1956 ████████████████████ Rev. Sun Yung Moon
and the Free-masons ████████████████████ with Ford Motors
glorious new empire ████████████████████ bigger than GM. GM was naturally
upset ████████████████████ ordered by the U.S. Army ████████
████████ young men died, sure, but ████████ automotive supremacy.
████████████████████

3: Vietnam War:
As the war raged, a young American ████████████████████
let's call him Bill ████████████████████ to Russia at the
time ████████████████████ on to Ho Chi Minh City
where he ████████████████████ with Jane Fonda, who
had firm, ████████████████████ like in Barbarella. ✓
At the time she had ████████ 10 ounces of the stuff ████████
on her ████████ Deng Xia Ping giggled ceaselessly ████████
████████ which led to ████████ and the fall of Saigon.

4: The Country of Your Choice: France
HUH? In 1995 we ████████████████████
████████████████████
████████████████████
████████ Operation: Jerry Lewis. ✓

(A+) Bravo! You've done it again.
By the way, has your father put any mor
thought to that Dept. of Ed. post?
                    —Prof. Schmaltz

** Summer Vacation Moving Sale**

- Halogen floor lamp $25
- Small fridge $35
      (good condition, slight cabbage smell)
- 4 Robotic killer squirrels $3.7 million
      (must provide good home)
- Vintage 1987 love-chair $10
      (good condition, needs springs, 2 legs)
- 6-pack of Meisterbrau (5 cans) $.75
- Kraft Macaroni+Cheese Cheese mix $.75

* Digital answering machine free with any purchase
   (contains heavy-breathing message from Newt Gingrich)

CHELSEA X8329 | CHELSEA X8329 | CHELSEA X8329 | CHELSEA X8329 | CHELSEA X8329 | CHELSEA X8329 | CHELSEA X8329 | CHELSEA X8329 | CHELSEA X8329 | CHELSEA X8329

Step right up, folks, step right up!
For only two bits
↪ SEE the fantabulicious GORE-GORE GIRLS
MARVEL at their blonde hideousness!
GASP at the blinding glare of their
      grotesquely white teeth!
AMAZE your friends and family
      with tales of a creature so
      monsterous, SO diabolical
      that the media had to love it!

Admission ¢5

THE ~ AMAZING
FREAKISH
GORE SISTERS

a: Homing pigeon
ansmission to: Quantico, Black Bag Division
om: California Dreamer

essage: Clinton Legal Defense Fund tapping dry.
Wire accrued interest from slush fund
in Caymens, acct. #H37C4-2; use to
pay down lawyers.

Further, let's wrap these hearings up.
Call Belgium 371-248, tell them
"Purple Horseshoes loves Al D'Amato."
Arrange for funeral wreath to be
sent to Mrs. D'Amato.
P.S. Inform Prez of what "he" did

HOW I STACK UP AGAINST OTHER FIRST KIDS

If I were born, like, a hundred years ago — then I'd be Chelsea McKinley or somebody.

THEM	THEIR ACHIEVEMENTS
Neil Bush	lost billions of $ in S&L scandal — my allowance is $50 a month; you do the math
Ronnie Reagan	Strutted his "stuff" on SNL — even his stuff couldn't make that show funny
Patti Reagan	Yeesh! Patti Reagan!
Ford's kid (what's her name)	Married her Secret Service agent — ugh, that's like kissing your brother
Spalding Taft	A reknowned twit

White House Documents

Look how small I am! COOL!

MOTEL 8

Dear Chelsea,

Your last letter & the enclosed gas ✗ really lifted my spirits. Sadly, my big tour of the greater Birmingham area ended abruptly last ~~week~~ night. The manager of the Chuck E. Cheese didn't want to pay the band, Chel. "A Karaoke machine ain't no band" is how he put it But I'll be damned if I let him insult my Lucinda like that. You ever seen blood bounce off an icy motel blacktop? It looks just like love.

How are you? You making whoopee? Chelsea? Hello? wait, this is a letter. You can't answer me, that'd be silly!!! He he he he ha ha ha ha ha ha ha ha ha piggie pie? HA HÄHA HA HA HA HA HA Could you swing me a music-teaching gig at Stanford? I'd sit in the back of the class & not bother anyone.

I really can't ask Bill for more favors. I'm starting to feel like the Fredo of the Clinton family. I'm not FredO. I'm not Fredo I just need to PULL myself up by my boot-straps & gain some WHOOPS! doorbell! Must be the harlots & rug-cleaning fluid I ordered. Gotta go, Leslie! Keep your nose clean, kiddo.

XXX, Uncle Roger

You never saw this. ok?

P.S. for references, I'm enclosing my just-finished rock-opera "A GRAVY LADLE Built for 2"

I have survived useless professors and their pointless knowledge.

I have survived a security-infested date.

I have climbed every mountain and forged every stream.

I have suffered the slings & arrows of outrageous politics.

And after all that,
I have emerged...

CHELSEA: WARRIOR PRINCESS

Tony,
If this book falls into the wrong hands and they decode page 7, ALL IS LOST!! destroy this book!

White House Documents

♫ Happy Trails to you . . . ♫

Chelsea's Handwriting: Mary Horenkamp

The Authors would like to thank:
Chelsea*
The Clintons
The Free Masons
Judith, Richard, & Nicole Eaton; Robert, Deonne, & Scott Jackson; Cathy, Marc, Dianne, & the Grand-Lendlers; Gus, Bonita, & George Boznos; Kerry Soper, Mary Horenkamp, Kevin Lang, David Cashion, The Good People of *Cracked* (Barry, Andy, Lou, & Cliff) and Globe Communications, Ilene Schechter, Ellen Topel, Dave & Alex/Howie, Pen Kojima, Cullen Duffy, Jason Torchinsky (for nuclear reactor help), Erin Miller, John Parnell, Rabbi David M., Martin McDonagh, Amy Ryan, Janet O'Connor, Grant Dawson, The Geppner, Birdie Hapner, Secret Service Tony, Nuclear Squirrel (1500 Series), and [your name here].

The Artist would like to thank:
His wife Lisa, his brother Stan, his whole family, Allen Tullos, the *Spoke* Editors: Jason, Todd, Holly, and Josh.

*Whom we sincerely hope has a wonderful time in college, and doesn't take this seriously.

ISBN 0-7868-8046-5

First Edition
10 9 8 7 6 5 4 3 2 1